GLIMPSES

POETRY BY

WILLIAM TORRIE KING

GRATITUDES

The birth of this book of "glimpses" has taken place in Northern Ireland, on the Antrim Coast. The mountains and sea, the quixotic sky and the verdant landscape, have provided a new and an ancestral background—affording a freshness of perspective.

I am grateful to the congregation of Covenant Presbyterian Church in Madison, Wisconsin, for giving me the time to write and for having shared so much of their jubilation and heartache with me over so many years.

Members of the faculty of the University of Wisconsin have been gracious in spending time with me to discuss the ethical issues that they have encountered in the pursuit of their disciplines.

Paddy McNeill has been our host in Ireland, teaching us the ways of the sea and the story of the land, and providing us with a magnificent cottage on the coast aptly named," John o' the Rocks."

Finally, I should like to thank Mary, who has the amazing capacity to become thrilled with mornings and excited about the wonders to be perceived in land and seascapes, and to sing out with joy at the discernment of yet another species of bird or flower. It is she that has read these writings for comment, encouragement and criticism. It is she that has been my enduring and loving partner for more than five decades; and it is to her that I dedicate this book.

If these "glimpses" provide you with some playfulness, pondering and encouragement to look at life with your own fresh insights and outsights; then I shall be well pleased.

As we say in Ireland: "all the best."

CONTENTS

Poems from Home in Madison

Poems from Cut Foot Sioux Cabin

PREFACE

The very mention of the word "Ethics" sends, if not a chill, at least a minor tremor, running down my back. It was my mother who used to ask with the gravity of a Supreme Court judge whether what I had just done was "ethical." Since she only posed the inquiry when what I had done was not remotely close to ethical, I have shied away from addressing the concept in later life. My background suggests that ethical is a term that one uses to assess another's deeds when one is quite sure that what he or she has just done—isn't!

Ethics seems to suppose that there are correct actions for the many circumstances that are encountered during the course of a day. Being ethical is a matter of matching the action with the circumstance, very much like the word games that list capitols on one side of the sheet and countries on the other, and ask us to draw a line to connect the related pairs.
Ethics, understood in this manner, has categories from which to draw. And these categories provide a vast array of pigeonholes in which moral circumstances can be filed, and with that the ethical understanding is provided.

However, it is often pretty difficult to discern the circumstance for which there is a preferred principle to be applied. It is deceptive to think that one is armed with the ability to apply what one has learned about justice or mercy or truth or love to the circumstances and situations of our lives. While such concepts as the ethical writings of theologians and philosophers write about, cultivate the highest forms of intellectual rumination; they have not served particularly well in terms of giving practical guidance. The principle is not the problem—the clear assessment of the circumstance is.

I have this suspicion that "ethical principles" are the reflections upon events that have taken place, rather than forecasters of what moral opportunities lie ahead. I don't think that we human beings are primarily rational. The nature of us is more to be found in our being communal. Our fullness of being, or lack of it; is expressed in how we relate to one another and to our world and to our god, rather than in private thought processes that hermetically seal us in actionless reason.

This does not mean that we are not rational. Nor does it claim that reason is unnecessary. The question concerns where reason enters the ethical process. And I do not think that this occurs at the beginning of it.

Ethics is founded, not in reason, but in perception. How one sees the world is the prime shaper of how one acts and how one thinks. Ethics is a matter of the heart.

How we perceive our circumstances has a great deal of influence on how we act. By circumstances, I mean more than the particular event that draws our attention and calls for a response: I mean the circumstances in relationship to the rest of the world in which we live.

The remarkable observations by scientists that a butterfly flapping its wings in China has an influence on the subsequent weather in the United States, liberates perspective from a single thread to a woven fabric.

Ethics is a matter of perspective: how we view the world in which we live. And this is a matter of conviction or belief.

In Scripture, Jesus is referred to as the Word that became flesh. The backdrop of this is the portrait of Joseph as an old man of highest moral standards and Mary as a young woman of purity. But neither Joseph nor Mary, by themselves, could create a child that could become the incarnation of the Word of God—that gift was bestowed by the Spirit of God itself.

When the word and the flesh were bonded together, the fullness of being was created. Jesus was the one who could and did relate to the whole of creation, giving birth to the ethics about which I shall try to write.

Jesus' parables are full of reversals. He starts the listener in one direction and gains attention by pointing out things that everyone knows. But, then comes the turnaround. Just when we know how the parable should end, Jesus takes us to an entirely different conclusion.

Jesus speaks often about the Kingdom of God. And when he does, he grounds it in the present and gift-wraps it in the future. He is talking about glimpses of life in its wholeness. Just now, glimpses are all we get, of a world that is knit together in wholeness and embraced by those that love it and can sense their belonging to it and rejoice in their participation in it.

Those glimpses are the occasions of communal ethics, of actions and thoughts called forth by the perception of reality that sees the world as a gift to be opened, a present to be shared, a joy to be celebrated.

This is in wondrous contrast to a principle-bound existence that looks upon life as an endurance course with the goal being that of getting through it with the fewest mistakes possible.

I shall try to write about the world of reversals, about the bonding of word and flesh, about believing as the precursor to seeing and about the glimpses of the Kingdom of God that people have shared with me.

Glimpses are better written in poetry than in essay, for a glimpse needs a sign aimed toward a reality that is both beyond and part of us. Poetry is a medium which points rather than makes a point.

The following gathering of my poetry contains reversals, glimpses, and an occasional "harrumph" at religion that atrophies the spirit.

The first poems were written on the Antrim Coast, in the company of a peat fire and a view of Scotland across the sea.

The second poems are the observations of life at home, in Madison, Wisconsin; where I have lived and worked and retired. I also have included "CECADE" in this section, which depicts a school in Peru, that is co-sponsored by the Downtown Rotary Club.

And the last section contains poems written at a cottage in the Chippewa National Forest at a lake named "Cut Foot Sioux."

ANTRIM COAST

ACCEPTANCE

I am accepted

As I am.

How nice.

But who is the "I"

That is being accepted

With such abandon?

I don't like all of me.

Is that part taken, too?

Or is it only the good

Or the bad?

Is it the bright and wise?

Or the dark and dumb?

Do not accept me so quickly.

You do not know me yet.

Take your time.

Let me be.

AGING

You can't walk as far or as fast.
Your body no longer stays up and in.
And you prefer dawn to midnight.
That means that you're growing old.

Someone must think that youth was better.
It is in my parting with it that I become aged.
But if those days were my epitome;
Why am I, in "olding", said to "grow?"

There is a wisdom that slowly comes,
Now that my body takes its moments.
Immortality is not my assumption
And waking into a new day is a gift.

"Growing" is a lovely course to take.

The longer we do it, the less we need carry.

Life is the discarding of the non-essentials.

And finally we are left with only the spirit:

Which is just how we began:

Except for the gratitude

That growing old has taught

And passed along.

BROODING

Like a bear awakening
From a winter's sleep
Comes an ancient fear
That I thought was gone.

Just a word or a look,
From someone unaware,
Has called it up again.
Anxiety has a new day.

Getting my life together
Is not an easy chore.
The pieces I've discarded
Make surprise returns.

When all is said and done—
Its not!
Hibernating doubt
Waits for another Spring.

CURTAIN CALL

Being made in the image of God
Is a most unlikely casting.
For we human beings
Who wish for comfort.

We have forgotten the script
And try to role-play
An unknown entity
In frantic pantomime.

Life would be a center stage
If we were not in its way,
And if we were to settle
For a supporting part.

Follow the east born star
And take delight in moments
When love is received
And given as well.

Seek intensity in aliveness.
It will serve us very well,
Bringing glee and gloom
To punctuate our call.

CUSHENDUN

This is a place of quiet tide.
There is no crashing boom
Of belligerent wave
Pounding out its presence.

This is a place of quiet tide.
There is no petulance
In the act of unwatering.
Rocks refresh again.

Which is better—tide in or out?
There is smoothness in the neap.
There is cragginess in the ebb.
They belong to each other.

This is a place of quiet tide,
Marking life by depth alone;
And finding certainty
In breath-like change.

DARK NIGHT

There he sat in front of the tube
With his mind mushed in homage
Of the blessed noise and color
That avoided thoughtfulness.

In front of his multi-channeled
Altar of escapism, remote in hand;
He worshiped as a voyeur:
Peeking at reality in pretense.

His body, a tired concertina,
Craved times to buy a machine
That would restore his youth
And let him dream again.

His god took the offering
By toll free number so that
He would not need to move
As he ordered a new self.

Is that all you're going to do—
Watch that thing all night?

It was the voice of boredom
From his semi-remembered partner.

She was tired from housework
That atoned for the fact that
Her career was elsewhere
And maybe her life as well.

At least there, busyness kept away
The great shadows of emptiness.
Tiredness became the antidote
For haunting life questions.

He dozed in his anger.
She made lists in hers.
And they went to bed
In different rooms.

They had made it. Success.
The dream was theirs.
And what was it, really?
A very long nothing at all.

DECENT

It is a gift to blush,
To be embarrassed,
To turn your head
And look away.

A nonplussed stare
In the face of evil
Is not a wise act,
Even if it is cool.

Without the grace
To be taken aback
At minor atrocities,
Virtue atrophies.

All that is left
Is a stub of a person
That takes pride
In not being offended.

If the standard used
Is whether I can handle it;
Then ethics collapses
Into endurance.

DISCREDIT

Another day of haunts
Tarnishes my satisfaction.
For everything I did,
There was more to do.

I do not understand
Why I feel morally bound
To discredit my life
With grandiose guilt.

Someday I should like
To hear a celestial voice
Declare: "well done,
O good and faithful one."

But if that did happen,
Then woe is me.
I probably would think
That God missed something.

DAWDLING

With a tip of a cap,
Or a wave of a hand,
Or the wag of the head,
Comes affirmation.

How different is a lane
From a harsh pavement
That has had removed
Its bends of civility.

Getting somewhere fast
Misses what is passed by.
It is earnest in avoidance,
Not cordial with encounter.

Sacredness is always in peril
When put up against efficiency.
There is a calling to dawdle
And measure in a different way.

A good journey is weighed
By encounter and wonder,
Not speed and independence.
One reaches the end soon enough.

DRAGON

Watch out for the dragon.
He sleeps by the surf
With his nose at the sea
And his back on the turf.

His eyes are well closed.
His wings wrapped around,
He lies there in his wait
For a ship to run aground.

He'd settle for a tasty man
But can't find one at all.
So he dozes now and dozes then
And waits in Cushendall.

DREAMS

Dreams are like a vessel dropped.
Its pieces cannot hold a thought.
Sharp edges stab the would-be gatherer.
Brokenness cannot be mended.

Dreams offer the shards of the day,
The littering of a broken world.
They nearly mimic the seen and done,
But leave cracks and gaps that stare.

Dreams come as little pranks
To the ordered self of the awake.
They poke fun at the all-togetherness
Of anyone who missed the mystery.

Dreams offer ill-formed haunts
That serve notice that our mind still hunts
For a peaceful world and quiet self
That never quite appears.

EMANCIPATION

There may come a moment
When the hurts of the past
Will no longer be carried
Into the world of today.

When that moment comes
There is a shuddering of the soul,
Because freedom is an unknown
And loyalty seems dangerous.

What will you do?
Where will you go?
What will others think?
To these, no answer is present.

All that is known
Is that life is fragile
And will bear no more hurt
Inflicted out of habit.

Like a child again, is she;
Learning to walk upright
And to look ahead,
Instead of down.

There will be some stumblings
But there will be uprisings, too.
It is all a convoluted journey
That asks only to be trusted.

EN GARDE

Flailing is an awakening
For preservationists.
Eyes open to on-guard
Wariness of the world.

News is heard with stealth.
The enemy is anticipated:
Whether traffic or spouse
Or forgotten appointments.

The sour disposition
That motivates fear
Of one's neighbor,
Promises long life.

To have defense

As the chief end of being,

Against all attackers,

Makes for alienation.

Being well-preserved

Is an admirable trait?

But not for a person.

It befits a pickle.

ENLIGHTENED

Silence is like a moral shadow,

Casting not darkness over life;

But giving backdrop to candles.

Little glimpses of wonder

Are more to be trusted

Than brassy beacons.

Candles are to be hunched over,

In need of a hand to protect them.

They require the help of the seer.

Outsights and insights join together

When a fragile light

Is joined by the shadow of silence.

FAULTLESS

She stood waif-like,
With no good words.
Her only comment
Was a single tear.

He spoke at last:
"I was tired,
Stressed,
Focused elsewhere.

"Don't blame me
For your upsetness.
Its your problem.
Pain is self-imposed.

"I am innocent.

The only hurt I claim

Is my very own.

Leave me alone."

The power to hurt

Is the power to heal

That has gone astray

In search of numbness.

FIRST LIGHT

With the first light of day
Comes awareness in subtle gray,
Stirring all that slept the night
With soft births of newfound sight.

FREEDOM

I awoke to the day like a Calvinist,

The bright clarity bringing forth a grimace.

Surely if the morn is filled with goodness,

With time things only will get worse.

There is handiness in cause and effect

Put together with equal shares of right and wrong.

If it begins good, it will end bad—

Or the reverse will be nearly as true.

We were well taught—do the difficult first,

And save the easiest to the last.

It's a very predictable way to stave off

Any perception of unexpected delight.

Someday, when I feel wickedly free,

I shall eat dessert for breakfast,

And do easy things for a while,

And wink at the God who winks back.

FRIENDSHIP

I have a best friend
Who takes me as I am.
There is no disapproval.
It's all without criticism.

I'm his best friend, too.
He can do what he wants
When he's around me.
I won't question him.

He likes what I like,
And he does what I do.
We can be ourselves
Without a conscience.
What a pity!

THE GAME

He was a thorough professional,

Conservative in dress,

Neat in appearance,

Punctual at meetings,

Aggressive in sales.

He talked of sports

And exotic toys

And thought himself to be

A most devoted family man..

That was earlier---

Before the pink slip

That announced the downsizing.

Evacuate the premises!

Clear your desk by noon.

Sorry—that's business.

Have a golden parachute.

You won't go hungry.

Is that what it was about?

Food?

GODFORSAKEN

Have you ever felt alone,

Most particularly when

There are people around

And they are connected

With some invisible strand

That you cannot find

Or try to grasp onto

Or even glimpse?

That is loneliness and

When it is stripped of any

Sense of righteousness

And defensive eliteness

Then it is the utter negation

Of any meaning or place

And there is nothing left

But to be Godforsaken.

Jesus was there.

GOOD WORKS

Today, I said to myself;

I shall set out to do some good.

So I got a bucket and went to the shore.

I picked up pebbles and filled the bucket.

So far, so good! The plan was clear.

The pebbles were for the road, which was rutted.

It was a fine job. It went on for hours.

At last it was done, and the road was smooth.

Today I have done some good, said I.

But then came the visitor, with badge and all.

I showed him the road: he asked about the shore.

And the next day I put the pebbles back.

Doing good is difficult.

The good here is the bad there.

Perhaps I'll start again.

But next time I won't use a bucket.

GROWING DOWN

It is strange:
Becoming naïve again.
Growing up equated caution
With maturity.

It was all very boring
But certainly prudent.
Insure everything and
Risk as little as possible.

Protect against all loss.
Preserve at all costs.
Nothing ventured: good!
Is there not a different way?

Become again as a little child.

Trust when you know better.

Risk when you might lose.

Love beyond a broken heart.

All of this invites growing

That approaches birth,

And welcomes an adult

Who has become a child.

GROWING UP

There is something warped

About looking inside ourselves

For news about eternal truth.

It brings a fascination to

Getting in touch with

Our very own inner child.

It might be better for all concerned

If we were to spend time

Looking outside ourselves.

We would find expectations

And hopes and fears

That make adulthood possible.

HALE-BOPP

The comet is in the skies this night
Hurtling tail-first out of sight,
Greeting all who look up high:
A silent force, a cosmic sigh.

How pleasant that it shines for me.
How charming that it glows for thee.
That it has come in our own age
Stamps blessings on our history's page.

Yet, what if it came all on its own
And seeks to eye us from its throne.
Its path crossed with a glimpse sublime
That watches us in its chosen time?

IMBALANCE

When I am free of guilt
I am out of touch with reality.
It is really hard to know
Whether to repent or enjoy.

Religious equations
Put Jesus on one side
And us on the other,
So that it all balances.

He died in innocence
We live in fallenness.
It evens the scales
And makes God fair.

How rotten I need to be
To make God look good
For turning away
From an only child.

What if we have it wrong
And God did not leave
And the child gave life—
The cross did not take it.

That's what the bible says,
But it is a dangerous book
For churches that need sin.

INSTINCT

Why did they kill Jesus?
He healed the lame and
Gave sight to the blind
And told the truth.

The god of preference
Rewards the strong
And keeps them very well.
Comfort displaces candor.

There's nothing like a god
That is made for one's own use.
And that's the problem with Jesus.
He didn't meet their needs.

They killed the God, who was,
To worship the one who wasn't.
You'd think they would have known.
Watch out for deadly instincts.

WROUGHT IRON

It was a good yard
With bricks to walk
And grass to watch.

Rows of spears on end
Were welded into immotion
Keeping the sky at bay.

The wrought iron
Wrapped the yard
In peered through privacy.

She used to watch the nuns
As they bustled by the fence
In starched habits and stiff shoes.

It was good that the fence was there.
It kept them out.
It kept her in.

It was like the old country,

The one she never quite left,

Where who you were not, was you.

Through the fence there was a glance

And it grew to a wave of the hand.

A "good morning" tumbled out.

And much to her own surprise

She answered the greeting,

Forgetting to be indignant.

The spaces in that fence were found

And hands reached out

To grasp a timid friendship.

The spears were unemployed.

JUSTICE

There sat the rest of the pie
With a third yet to be eaten.
We both had a yen for the rest
And settled on half for each.

But when it was cut, it was uneven.
He got more and I got less.
It's not fair, I fiercely sobbed.
Its not the way it should be.

But mother said, that final judge:
He's bigger and needs more.
And being fair is not the same
As being just—so there!

LIBEL

There is a severity to the church
As it seeks to remind us of our lostness.
It blesses us with sincere words
About how despicable we are
In the presence of our Creator.

What sort of madness is this?
If god is our creator, and despises
The creation: okay;
We all have bad days.
But don't blame me for it.

The preacher grimaced about love
And told us about blood spilled for us.
Fortunately, god's anger is sated
Because his innocent son is killed.
We sang: how great thou art.

I am trying to forgive the god portrayed,
For the blaming tirades and twisted
Benevolences that were pulpited.
I hope that the living God will not sue
For the slandering of her name.

LIMITED

Everything is spoiled
Because it will end,
And so it is tainted
With terminality.

They say I am born to die,
And that is all of that.
Why bother to live at all
If it won't forever last?

Value is in permanence.
That makes for futility
If one has the misfortune
Of having been birthed.

Here's some weird news:
Only what is passing away
Has purpose here and now:
So cherish it well.

LOVE

Love is not the sort of thing
Into which you dive or fall.
It is not a gooey quagmire
Of too clingy sentiment.

Love is not a dotage.
It is not adoration
Of one's self-wishes
Mirrored by another.

Love is a bond of freedom
That offers a safe haven
For one to be simply real,
And to find that held sacred.

Love is being beside oneself
And fully with the other,
And in all of that, to be at last,
To one's own self, most welcome.

MATURITY

There he sat in the judge's chair,
Making kindly comment about her:
Hair, posture, figure, weight—
And she was early flattered by it.

In time she wearied of ornamental praise.
In time he felt betrayed by her humanness.
She grew in frustration.
He mourned in loneliness.

He became abandoned, a married widower;
And she turned angry, a bridal bauble.
All they saw in each other
Was an absence of themselves.

With the tenacity of a promise made
That was far from understood,
They began to learn of each other
And in time, love grew up.

MEMORY

It is curious indeed

That life is recalled by death.

Old men wear caps of battle

And medals from wars.

There are bold monuments

That honor the sacrificed,

But minor cemeteries for the rest.

Wouldn't it be enlivening

If we remembered kindnesses

And recorded history by them?

It would be truly amazing

To see a march of life veterans

Wearing---party hats.

MOURNING

John writes of a tie that
Binds us to a world
We cannot see.
How odd.

She died years ago.
I still remember.
A new closeness
Has set in.

Our past is being redone.
Hurts become insights.
Silences are broken.
Love gets easier.

The tie that binds
Is not a burden.
It is a hand offered
And gladly taken.

There is time after death
To finish the thought
And cherish the gone.
The tie is another chance.

MYSELF

Today I shall be dad
And read the morning news.
Today I shall be mom
And write the monthly dues.

Today I shall be sister
And talk about the boys.
Today I shall be brother
And think about my toys.

Today I shall be myself
And play and run around.
Today I shall be only me
And gladly leap and bound.

NEW AGE

Tradition is such a bother,
Always fussing to make sure
That everything that it does
Is precisely as it always was.

It is great to live in a time
When everything is new
And we have perfect license
To do our very own creation.

Each day is its own volume,
Not history bound to ancients.
This is liberating, a free fall
Into my own self-interest.

One slight trouble, though:
With nothing to lean on,
No memory or vision—
The books keep tumbling down.

THE ORCHESTRA

When the piece is completed
And the audience applauds
And the conductor bows
And soloists step forth:

Something else happens,
That is almost an aside.
The stars turn and nod
To the behind them players.

The wise ones know,
That if it were not
For brass and wind
And strings and drums

A concert would not be.
That is why
God is well thought of
As the accompaniment.

OVERCAST

Grey skies hold down eyes,

Giving no invitation

To look beyond the earth

Or peek at puffs of pretend.

There is solemnity in the day

For it gives no hint of sun.

It leaves such visions

In the vestibule of memory.

Grey skies impose patience

And the time for ordering

All that has been overlooked

In the squints of brightness.

The limits of the sky hold down.

They restore boundaries

And make pausing active.

Reverie has its own day.

OWNERSHIP

The mountains are so steep

That one could not climb them

Without resorting to all fours.

An upright stance would not do.

What is absolutely amazing

Is not so much the vertical incline,

But the fact that someone

Has built stone fences on it.

And sometimes, running next to it—

Is another fence just like the first,

To honor a generations-old

Border dispute that continues.

Fences can be works of art,

Stone locking into crevice,

Angle embracing angle,

Layer upon layer.

It is befuddling to think of the work

And the rocks carried up grade

And the life portion expended

Just to draw a stony line;

So that all that is on this side

Is no one's to touch or use

Because it belongs to the rock-bound

And there is a fence to prove it.

No foreign sheep will invade.

No one else will tread the grass,

Which no hand ever sowed

Nor could cause to grow.

A mountain with stone fences

Is like love with conditions.

It finally decimates the wonder

Of one more God-given gift.

PROMISES

Rubber bands are useful things.

They bind and hold and store

And keep together all that

They surround.

Rubber bands are lovely things.

They make music in boring places

And launch paper missiles ceiling-ward.

Rubber bands are dispensable.

They become a bracelet of indecision

For those who can not quite

Throw them away.

Rubber bands are promises made

That are kept beyond practicality

And shaped by what they keep

And who keeps them.

A PSALM

Joy starts in the toes.
It is the first touch
Of the body with the earth
From whence it came.

Joy is a connectedness
With the lived-in world.
It is the naming of the animals:
Addressing them politely.

Good morning, earth and sky
And grass and trees
And birds and fish
And dogs and sheep.

Joy is greeting the household

And the neighborhood,

And the community

With a belonging affection.

Joy is the pleasantness

Of thanking God

For glimpses of oneness

Throughout the earth.

PUT

Sitting in a chair, where I was put,
And trying to remember why I'm here;
Eating blandness with a spoon
And given orders by piped-in sound:

This is my retirement home.
I am given prolonged uselessness.
Once I did things for others.
That was when I was of worth.

Why this? Death would be simpler.
Must I continue on as such a bother?
The children make their pilgrimage
And each of us is made uncomfortable.

Could it be that this is a new calling,

A chance to minister with gratitude,

To give thanks for simple things

That once I could do?

Has God saved this great humbling

For the days of aged wisdom?

Perhaps true thanksgiving

Is beyond the very young.

RECONCILIATION

Be consistent, he told himself;
That is the way of all good parents.
Don't go back on your word,
No matter how mistaken it was.

She had listened, hurt and puzzled,
To the orders to go to her room.
She had taken blame for nothing
That she had done—and wept.

He sat in his chair, trying to make wrong
Into something right and principled:
But it wouldn't work. The lie sputtered,
And his heart ached with shame.

He went to her door, with fear unchecked,
And mumbled about how sorry he was.
She burst forth with forgiveness.
They hugged and grace had its moment.

REPRIEVE

As the sun warms the air
Great plumes of mist
Are sent to the hillside,
Swooping upward like a freed bird.

Clouds envelop the village
Like a blanket nestles a child,
And everything is rescued
From a too early awakeness.
Morning gets a reprieve.

RIGHTEOUSNESS

Do what is right!
That is the calling
Of any person
In this world.

But what is right?
The tradition I was taught
That has left us tattered
With supremacy—

Or the great principles
That are full of logic
That don't make sense
In the here and now—

Or whatever I feel
That is self-affirming
Even on the days that
I don't trust me?

What is right?
God only knows,
And so I'll settle
For a bit of kindness.

THE ROCK

Rocks don't do anything.
They just sternly stay put
And the water comes to them
And at high tide washes over.

Sometimes there are waves
Which pound against the icon
And sometimes only lap,
Each having its own pilgrimage.

If time is counted by ages
And not the hours of clocks;
Then the rocks are shaped
By all that has come to them.

O God my rock and my redeemer,
It is the saga that brings me close,
And quickly alters what I am.
Are you, my rock, changed as well?

SALVATION

The sea awakens from tranquility,
Stirred by the goading of the wind.
Whitened foam rides along the top
Of curling crests of ocean waves.

There is no coyness in this bed of water,
No currents in deceptive guise,
No muted encroachment by the tide,
No timid lapping upon the shore.

The wind is like the spirit—dawning
With power to bring senses alert,
Displacing calm with boldness
And overturning inattentiveness.

Call upon the wind of God to come
And you will be shaken with aliveness.
There will be nothing left the same,
For you will be rescued from the calm.

SEA PINK

Audacity in light red
Is the color
And disposition
Of the sea pink.

It grows in unlikelihood,
Gathering the stuff of moss
From the sweepings of the sea
Over intensely craggy rocks.

It is so out of place,
On its divot of green,
Impudently perched on
The most severe of stones.

The way in which to disarm
The militancy of harshness
Is simply to become a flower
With joyful impertinence.

THE SHEPHERD

I used to love the 23rd psalm
With the great shepherd imagery.
That was when I lived in the city
And had never met a sheep.

I liked being a wooly lamb
Cradled in Gods own arm,
Carried home from lostness
And lifted out of harm's way.

Now that I've met a sheep or two
And watched the playful lambs,
I wish the Lord were not my shepherd
For I'd like not to be a ram—or ewe.

Perhaps the problem is not God
In the metaphor of shepherd.
It just might be that I've self-inflated
And ought to be more sheepish.

STRESS

Stress is what they call it.
It is a grand new ailment,
And for a blessed economy
There are remedies at hand.

If you will take this or do that;
Ingest some pills and soak
Or sit like a pretzel and hum,
Then tranquility will descend.

I think the name's all wrong.
Stress is not the ailment.
We consume too much of life
By being grandly busy.

And hope that by raising dust

We will prove our worth.

But that gnaw of non-meaning

Persists in all the work,

What if we did less and just enjoyed

Our place in life and on the earth,

 And depleted our busyness

Instead of the planet.

TEETER TOTTER

What is heavy goes down.

What is light goes up.

Each needs the other

In the world of teeter totter.

Bad faith is the board upon which we sit

That weights us with sins galore.

The lower we sink, the higher god goes

And we both have a tenuous time.

Good faith is not a children's game.

It is a walk through a long lost Eden

With the God who has come to join us

In searching for sacred growings.

The Creator is not up—we are not down.

The plank is left and the journey begun.

The garden guide is always with us,

And together we discover life,

Hand in hand.

TERRITORY

Nature also mourns a lost good.

So said the apostle Paul. Perhaps

While he was watching birds,

The gull and the red shank.

Both want the piece of the ocean

That is claimed by the oystercatcher.

When one moves, the other pounces.

Each spends the day wishing

That it was where the other is.

The victory of one is made possible

By the absence of the other.

So much for natural good

And hoping at its dumbest.

THEOLOGY

The ocean is too big to own,
And in its size it is humbling.
It is good to look at the sea
And reflect with modesty.

Where land has been left dry
It stops abruptly with a cliff,
Or meanders with abandon
To the coast which it becomes.

Standing on the highest ground
The expanse brings marvel
That is coupled with the fear
Of falling off the edge.

Wading along the shore
Gives no offering of grandeur
And there is no dread
In sand between the toes.

Life has its waders and walkers
Immersing themselves
Or digging in their heels.
Each has found the sea.

TOXIC TALK

I can say what I please:
That's real freedom.
Words are only words.
They do no good nor harm.

Perhaps that goes too far.
Words to another have cost.
They offend or inform
Or hurt or even heal.

But words to myself,
That's a different matter.
I can say what I want.
No one else will know.

My sayings become my seeings.
It is the price of speech,
And if my words are care-less,
Will I be that as well?

TREE

What are you doing?

Cutting down this tree.

Why?

It's in my way.

Why don't you go around it?

It takes too long.

Are you in a hurry?

Always.

Why?

Life is short.

Especially if you are a tree.

THE TROUBLES

Like a damp shroud draping
The once clear mountain,
So come ancient hurts
That seek to bury the spirit.

That cloud, once sky-lightened,
Is now a tearful sogginess.
Like a well-cried handkerchief
It serves only as a memory.

And the high ground is no guide
For lost ones to find their way.
It only rises to block the path
To an unfound destination.

If the sky were to clear

And the mountain could again

Mark the way home,

Then each would honor the other.

The green would look up

And the white would look down,

And all of earth's traveler's

Would be safe again.

TRUCE

Peace is what is longed for

Or so it is claimed.

But what is peace?

Is it only the end of war?

Because there are no bullets

Or armored cars

Or strafing planes

Hurtling.

Does that mean that there is peace?

Do not view the machinery,

The technology of war,

In its quietness, as bliss.

Peace is a change of heart.

It is the fearsome claim

That your life is worth

More than mine.

And I must trust that

You believe that, too.

Peace needs to be a verb

And put into action.

Cheap threats will terror bring,
But not a new heart and right spirit
About which the psalmist sung.
Peace is to be embraced, not enforced.

So throw away the arsenal-minded.
Silliness of quieted weaponry.
It is not the age for which we long.
It is no more than a carnal pause.

Do peace with your neighbor.
This is not your world to zone
Like sheep behind stone fences.
Do peace and tumble the rocks.

Shudder at the price to be paid
For the cost is humility and
The reward is a small thing—
Gratitude for another's life.

UNGODLY

To order the stars
And divide the lands
And have a plan
For everything:

That is the job of God
--Or so I thought,
Until chaos appeared
In my emerging world.

There is too much hurt
And active wrongness
For the celestial one
To right it all.

Perhaps there is no print
Of what the world will be,
No Deus Ex Machina in charge,
And we are on our own.

A far more irritating thought
Is of a redefined power
Where God joins us in struggle,
Vacating the heavenly throne.

A most peculiar God, this one,
Who finds power in a love
That tends to break hearts,
Creating unexpected nobility.

WAITING

There it stood
In polite dormancy.
Branch upon branch
Giving no hint of life.

There is a futility
In growing impatient
In the wait for sap to rise
And leaves to sprout.

Waiting is an art form,
Calling for a stillness
That is warmed with hope
And quieted with promise.

When admiration is learned
For the tree standing empty,
The preparation is complete
For the fullness of Spring.

THE WALK

They walked down the beach
Holding hand upon hand,
Letting go to skip stones
And write in the sand.

Each needs the other both less and more
As the path grows long and memory wide.
They have come to love what they do not know
Of their partner's deep and sacred side.

The stones they skip will pause and sink.
The clasp they hold will fail the hand.
But the walk they took, to talk and think
Will far outlast those steps in sand.

THE WIND

The winds of the day came blowing in
As gusts of power that battered all
That dared to face its strength
And stand in bent unmovedness.

But some were like the gulls
Who greeted the force as a friend.
They set their wings to meet its thrust
And flew to heights beyond themselves.

Those who stood in fierce resistance
Spent all the day in stationary combat
And measured life by their own fatigue.
They missed being airborne altogether.

Meet the forces of life as friends, gifts:
And you will fly right over yourself,
Soaring and gliding in ways far above
Hunched over wheezes of endurance.

WRINKLES

What rhymes with wrinkle?
I asked myself in the mirror.
Words like twinkle crinkle
And tinkle came to mind.

I splashed water on the face
To see if it would remind
My skin of where it belongs.
Now I had wet wrinkles.

Why do I look at me and try
To find whom I once was.
I think and feel the same,
As luminous as always.

I look like a melted candle,
And this seems strange.
Flames consume, spend.
Why should I look unkindled?

O God, bless me with wrinkles
And let the marks of a lifetime
Be the beautiful comments
Of well used gratitude.

0

HOME IN MADISON

ADOPTED

We are the adopted children of Israel:
So says the apostle Paul.
Then what about the church?
Is it our home or our orphanage?

I like the latter, not the former.
Church is not a spiritual bunker
Where I can escape life's anguish,
And find solace within the family.

Church is an ecclesiastical launch pad.
It is there I find direction and purpose
It is in there that I find the courage to go
Out into God's world—my new home.

BRUISES

Sometimes, when a chair
Or vicious leg of table
Rises up and smites me:
It hurts a lot
And foolishes me
In my attempt to blame.

There is a lingering ache
After the collision
That is known only by
My body and my self.

But later on, like ships' colors;
My body posts yellows and
Purples and blues and blacks.
By then the hurt is over.

But just then is when others see
And inquire about the bash—
Sometimes more interested in
The how of it than the to whom.

Contusions are curious.
They appear when they don't hurt
And are hidden when they do.
Sometimes life is like that—
A bruise too late in showing.

CECADE

Cradled in the arms
Of the valleyed Andes
Awaits a well-spring of hope,
Welcoming the yearners.

Be surrounded with its gentleness
And remember a long-forgotten past.
Be lifted up with newness
And learn the "could be" of a bright future.

This is the place of tangible wonder
Where strands are spun into readiness
And the threads are gathered together,
Weaving life into the fabric of joyful purpose.

Come to the well-spring of hope
And discover the world all over again.
Go home by a new way on an old path
And greet life with compassion and delight.

COMPASSION

When the hands that were held
Become the hands that hold;
When help once given
Becomes help returned;
Then grace is complete.

Life is startled by generosity.
It is awakened by giving.
It is gentled by receiving.
To share in plenty and want
Is the gift of companionship.

There is a terrible aloneness

That is fostered by independence;

The self-cursed soul that needs nothing,

Nor gives anything,

Withers with inhumanity.

What better to learn than

The art of holding hands.

Entwined fingers provide

The birthplace of love

And compassion set free.

CORDLESS

Right in the midst
Of a pre-bed doze
The phone went off,
Sounding like the
Awful music that
Gets played at me
When I am put on
Hold with the promise
That my call is really
Important.
My new phone is not corded.
It hides in the couch,
Or under the paper,
Or on the bathroom shelf.
With startled urgency
The thing was found,
And a strange voice
Asked if I were me.
It then wanted to know
If I had an illness for
Which it was offering
A wonderful cure.

I tried to hang up.

Without my glasses

I pawed at buttons

Until the voice stopped.

My old phone was coiled.

I always knew where it was.

My old phone knew me

And didn't offer a cure

Or aluminum siding

Or burglar alarms.

And the old phone

Had a place to be

And a politeness

Of silence,

When put back

In its holder.

Life needs cradles

And anchors

For holding safe

Sacred things.

DEEP BREATH

It happens in the Exam room
When the doc professionally says:
"Take a deep breath."
I do—it's like an inverse yelp.

Sometimes it happens in a marriage.
Life together erodes into mutual tasking—
It functions well—and that's the all of it.
Those times call for a deep breath.

The inhalation provokes a shudder
And senses its own powerlessness.
It is the death of the way it was,
Giving way to a labored breath.

Take a deep breath
And get married again.
It's like a breath of fresh air
Re-inflating life together.

DROUGHT

Parched is what it is, and who we are.

All that lives withdraws into itself.

Survival overwhelms compassion,

And nature, too, mourns a lost good.

The soul of a nation dries up as well

When the drops of tearful sorrow

Fail to fall for the underclassed

While the privileged sprinkle their lawns.

We are in the very midst of drought,

Waiting for the blessed moisture

That will awaken life to love

And wash away the dust of indifference

Come, o come, you waters of life.

Rain away our parchedness.

Let our tears flow from our spirits set free.

Then our deepest dryness shall be

quenched.

DOWNLOOK

Taking the dog for a walk
On a daily travelled path
Which has been well-hidden
With snow-covered ice;
Starts with a furtive look
At the park benches that mark
The distance to be traversed.
That's the outlook that sees
That it is too far, too hazardous'
And that I am too old.
As the dog waits patiently
I look down and see a print
From an earlier sojourner
And putting a boot into it,
I seek another and another
And another and another.
The bench greets us both
And the walk completes.
It was the outlook that sighted
The goal, and the downlook
That led the way.

ECHO

I looked at her

And saw her disappearing,

Slipping through my hands of well-gnarled love

Like quicksilver scattered by a grasp.

I looked at her and listened to her same words over again.

Why were the thoughts new to her?

Did she not remember?

Was she misplaced?

I looked at her and she fell deep inside herself.

I was still with her, but she was fading,

    Spiraling

        Into

            A

                Deep

                Canyon

        Of

      Forgetful-

Ness.

I looked at her

And she seemed pleasantly puzzled.

She had become a stranger to her own home

And could not find her way back again.

I looked at her

And spoke to no one I could find.

How can it end like this:

With only an echo of a soul gone empty?

FOR BETTER AND WORSE

Talk to me; tell me the world is getting better.

Whisper to me: tell me the world is getting worse.

Boast to me about the miracles of modern man.

Cry to me about how good it used to be.

I hear it all: the better and worse, the now and the then.

None of it is particularly convincing.

The past of righteousness does not find support in history.

The present as enlightenment does not bear out.

Better it is, I think, to look at this world as a heartbeat.

Sometimes the constriction, sometimes the expansion—

Always pumping, but never really getting anywhere.

That is the story of morality left to humankind.

But then, just before despair talks me into giving up;

I hear giggles from children, and sobbing from old people,

And resolve from ghost-infested

And welcomes from long-time loners.

Life is a symphony of pulses. It is a surprise of phoenixes.

It is the presence of angels in the midst of a garbage dump.

Life is a dance about what cannot quite be,

Accompanied by the world that never quite was.

FORGIVENESS

Forgiveness is a strange sort of thing.

It is God-required in the Lord's Prayer.

I don't much like the news that

I will be forgiven as I have forgiven.

I don't mind pardoning when the perpetrator

Comes appealing to my gracious nature.

But who does God think she is—telling

Me what I must do to win her favor?

Where's all of that unconditional love stuff?

IF ONLY GOD

If only God had a plan for homeland security

We might have been spared all of the fuss

About an infant that would grow to Saviorhood.

Instead we would have cosmic wiretapping

That knows when we have been naughty or nice.

If only God had a plan for the economy

We would not need bailouts or foreclosures

Or organic chickens or petroleum problems.

Instead we would bask in the earth's bounty

Made for our consumption and indulgence.

If only God had a plan for acting almighty,

We would not have to wage any more wars

On those who challenge our ways.

Instead we could humbly accept their desire

To be almost as good as we are.

But God didn't do these things.

Instead we are handed a little child

And told that in our caring for it

We will find the real plan for humanity:

Cradling God with tenderness.

IN ABSENTIA

Sometimes the morning

Lays an enveloping cloud

Of estranging mist

Right on top of all we knew.

What we had hidden

With careless familiarity

The fog came, and took it all away;

And there we were, all alone.

What other way is there

To treasure again

What surrounds and accompanies,

Than to have it taken away.

Piece by piece, eyeful by

Eyeful, the sun brings it back

And it is the same—but we are not.

Absence gives presence its meaning.

JELLO SALAD

The main symbol of wonder

At the old church suppers,

Which always ran out of

Deviled eggs too soon;

Was the jello salad. It showcased

Bits of fruit almost floating

In an encapsulating mold.

On special occasions there

Were little marshmallows

That were lifesavers near

But beyond the grasp

Of the desperate grape.

Jello salads are a great icon

For lifeless religion that

Mistakes "never changing"

For faithfulness, and misses

Altogether the delight

Of a living savior who grows

In wisdom and in stature.

KER-PLUNK

Take a small stone

Drop it from a tall place

Overlooking some water,

And it will go Ker-plunk.

The noise begins the concentric,

Those circles of water that grow

And look for the containment

Of an all-embracing shoreline.

Sometimes they end with a sigh on sand,

And other times with a yell on rock.

But always they stop when the shore is met,

And the expansion ceases forever.

We had a divorce in our family:

And guess what—

It went Ker-plunk

And we became the shore.

LIMITED WARRANTY

The Lord's Prayer is very handy

When said out loud and in a group.

Some say "debts" and others "trespasses."

Some end with "deliverance from evil"

And others add "power and glory."

Nobody notes that if we forgive others,

God will forgive us. But if we don't:

God won't forgive us either.

Nobody adds that except Matthew.

God freely forgives if we do.

If we don't, God doesn't.

That doesn't do much for an image

Of almightiness and all lovingness

And all the other alls of worship

That seek to write the job description

Of the one we worship.

God, whose ability to forgive, is limited

By our willingness to do the same—

That's awe-full!

MORE

Anybody knows

That more is better.

Better than what?

That's simple:

More is better

Than less.

More square footage

Of home and self

More money and credit,

More debt and interest—

This is the heartburn of

Indulgence.

Gorging is not limited

To thanksgiving:

It is a national pastime,

A tribute to a democracy

That consumed its very own

Freedom,

While chanting the new mantra:

"I deserve it."

NINE ELEVEN

It started like any Tuesday

With practiced careless exasperations

Of what the president said

Or congress didn't do

Or the stock market foreshadowed.

And then we heard: a plane crashed,

And into the World Trade Center.

Computer error? Altimeter wrong?

And then another plane—crashed as well.

What's happening, we said.

Apparently terrorists, they said.

And then, again: plane crash—the pentagon.

And once more, in Pennsylvania.

We froze. No flights. No stocks.

No smart-alecky comments about W.

No sneers at congress.

As the towers crumbled, falling in on themselves

A galvanizing pain emerged from a nation

Of hapless individualists.

And from death we began, again, to be reborn:

Rescuing

Grieving

Coming together

Searching

Resolving

And readying for an answer to war.

A cozy self-absorption is now gone

And freedom is being redefined

By stern limits.

ORIENTATION

Look to the east
And you will find
In the beginning of the dawn
The dayspring of life itself.

Look to the east
And turn away from dying night.
You will find light
In the first shyness of dawn.

Look to the east
And greet the sunrise
With the freshness of hope,
The clarity of a good promise.

Look to the east
And let go of the dreads
That makes you face the dark.
Behold the rising and rejoice.

POLITE

I remember the days
Of "please" and "thank you."
Their unspokenness could
Lead to the principal's office,
Or to home quarantine.
Manners were expected.

Times have changed---some
Would declare it moral evolution.
We are liberated from the "sirs
And "ma'ams" of yesteryear.

Freedom of speech has become
Mumbling disregard. Honor is
Lost and so is civility. It makes one's
Neighbor not someone to be loved,
But an object to be "whatevered."

Politeness is not well replaced by:
"How's it going, Dude?"

SITTING IN THE SUN

Sitting in the sun on a summer's day
Sat the children of life about to play.
The boys were on one side, all in a row
And the girls on the other with furrowed brow.

Each called to the other to come and play
Each called the other to do it their way.
And so they jeered and taunted all day long,
Each yelling without thought or song.

And so the day was spent, with no retreat
From curb to street, no new friend to meet.
And there they sat until the day grew tired
And evening watched as their taunts expired.

So it ended, this self-righteous game
With no clear winner and not any fame.
The fear of those on the other side,
Left each with only lonely pride.

TURNING TEEN

I'm pretty convinced

That anyone who says

That they wish they were my age—

Never was.

I wake in the morning with a mild case

    Of self-disgust

        Or cautious delight

            Or wondering who I really am.

My home is sometimes strange:

All goes well if I pretend to be

    A little girl

        Which I am not any more.

And if I declare my semi-grown-upness

Everybody rolls their eyes.

Its all pretty curious.

Life goes on and so do I:

    Puzzled and loved,

        Certain and loving.

And that is enough for the journey.

WAKE UP CALL

There was something mysterious
About that old mattress and spring.
It never tolerated major separations.
It squeaked with occupancy
And valleyed in the middle;
So that aloneness was not possible
And silence was not allowed.

I miss the old bed, now replaced by foam;
The kind that has a memory and
Conforms itself to me or me to it.
I am bubble-packed in isolation
For a "perfect" sleep; unmoved
By a turning partner
Or a cranky coil.

Some say our lives are suspended
By memory foam sensibilities.
It is a world defined by the "I"
That is endlessly entitled to what
It desires: walled off from others
By an undisturbed self. I miss the old bed
And the civility that came with it.

WIDOW'S FIRE

They called it a widow's fire

For it was small—and seemed to be

One log, all alone.

But they could not look

With the learned tenderness of solitude

And so they could not see

The snuggled partner there.

Life goes on in strangeness

Kindling quiet courtship.

Beneath the sole round,

Burning long and well

Is still the other,

Hidden in the ash of time.

Warmth was held safe.

VEINS

Don't talk of love with your veins popping out.

Tunnels of blood pumping in the neck

Are not the harbingers of benevolence.

I worry about love that is predicated

By an ecclesiastical knee in the groin.

Super Christians are so soul-swept

By the crucifixion

That they are clueless about the news

That he rose from the dead.

How strange to yell about Jesus

Dying for our sins

And forget all about him rising

So that we could have abundant life.

Put your veins back in

And love a little.

You might be amazed at the gospel.

CUT FOOT SIOUX CABIN

AUTUMN

It started with a basswood—
A stirring, willowy youngster;
Too busy being to fuss about becoming.
It was a sapling in a forest of permanence.

But then it happened—shyly at first.
One of its leaves awoke all yellowy.
Soon it was followed by its tree mates:
Alone together in a forest still green.

From this youth came news of autumn.
Constancy was transformed by change.
Life shed its visionless notion of endlessness,
While peering at death for the very first time.

BUDDIES

It is strange indeed

To grow old among friends.

They disregard our practiced laments

That declare that we can't do "it" any more.

They remember who we were

And expect us to be who we are.

What we can do is more interesting

That what we can't. They prefer

The presence of the present, and not

The absence of the past. Oldness is a

Gift to be shared with friends, so that

Each can cherish the other with

Well-gnarled love.

COLUMBINE

There is a flower that bows its head
With graceful beauty, all muted red.
Its stem grows up and peers at last
At earth-clung roots that keep its past.

Walk and run and dance around
But keep your feet not far from ground.
No future dream brings hope to last
Without a memory of its past.

So watch the flower that bows its head
With graceful beauty, all muted red.
It gives a glimpse of life divine
The now and then of the columbine.

FOG

Sometimes there is a fog

That quietly envelops the world;

Tucking it in,

Like a goodnight blanketing

Of a sleeping child.

It is the now of seeing dimly

And the pause that grants time

Before the face to face

Of a newborn day.

HANGNAIL

Every once in a while
It annoyingly appears,
And clings to its calling—
Which is: to annoy!

It is little and ugly and
Gets in the way.
It is a tactile barb that gives an "ouch"
To a welcoming touch.

Outside of me
It is a hangnail.
Inside of me it is guilt.
Both are nuisances
That pester life.

Sometimes, grace is
Like a nail clipper,
Snipping off lifeless
Bits of old haunt;

Taking away the power
Of a relived past

ICE MELT

The lake is parting

With its winter blanket.

The ice is going out.

There is the sweat of

Sun melt

And the groan of

Wind blown sheets

      Being pushed over

           Each other.

There is a sparkling

Tinkle of shore-lined

Particles, undulating

      By the nudge of

           Set free waves.

The waters of death

And life

Are mingled together by

Breath and warmth.

Change is birthed

And wonder is granted.

JOY

Sometimes joy is severely challenged

By old dogs marking territories

That include anywhere in the house

That they happen to choose:

Or by the old coffee pot that takes on

The disposition of Vesuvius,

Spewing grounds and hot water

All over the kitchen counter.

But that is joy for you,

With its puckish delight

In hiding behind a minor displacement

Of order,

To teach us to laugh

At the slight chaos which lurks

At the threshold of a new day.

NATIONAL SYMBOL

The hummer is an obnoxiously lovable

Beast. It postures at its feeder

Inflating its micro chest

On guard to the right and

Left. It quickly takes enough

Energy to make life miserable

For its feathered peers.

And then it returns to guard and

Drink. So goes its day—useless I think.

For all it exemplifies:

It might as well be our national bird.

ONCE

Once it was thought that newness
Was a blustery, bright and startling thing.
Once there was curious indignation,
Grumbling about how a good God could let
Our world collapse upon its own perversity.

Once people were wind-swept and parched
With anxious, semi-muffled disapprovals
That echoed with emptiness.

Anyway that was a long time ago,
Before reality settled in,
And hardened life into practicalities,
And taught stoic responses of
"That's the way it is,"
Strangely making friends with despair.

How curious that a teen-aged woman
And an old handyman
Have answered,
With most limited awareness,
What no one knew how to ask.

Newness is found in a straw-filled manger
That has all the powerlessness of a child
Who draws us near, and makes our embracement
Part of the re-creation.

A swaddled voice has whispered news
About a new world that almost happens;
But remains slightly elusive
So that faith must cling to the not yet.

Somehow, even though everything is the same,
It is all very different,
Because in the midst of our severe humanness,
God has chosen to join us.

OUTSIDE IN

I can turn my shirt inside out

And my inner child

Can come blithering about.

My deepest doubts I wear

Like a sweatshirt to hide

My very soul.

I like to be defensive when

I've got something to defend,

But benign indifference

Which is nonplussed to the max,

Is not a virtue, but emptiness.

I worry about Googling for my

Inner self, and trolling for information

Instead of seeking a bit of truth.

I pods and blackberries and yahoo and

All of that, are intriguing: but they

Ought not be the authors of my being.

Knowledge is information well digested

And ordered by who I am and will be.

It is the outside brought in,

And not the inside pilloried by instant info.

RADIO FLYER

There is something about a "Radio Flyer"
That brings back thoughts of speed and daring,
Of one-footed propulsion and long-handled
steering:
 Pulling, pushing, coasting—the way of the wagon.

And so it was that I parked it by the
Woodpile, resolutely shoving in log upon log .
 Pyramiding the load—So one trip would do.
Then I tugged the handle and off we groaned.

Halfway there we were, the Flyer and I,
When it took its leave of the chore.
Rescuing perspective by rolling on its side
And restoring the stack to logs by ones.

Sometimes life is treated like a too-full wagon,
stacked and pulled with grunting urgency,
Straining to do too much of too little,
And missing the thrill of riding the Flyer.

REALITY

Sometimes, in the dawned morning;

The lake, in quiet reflectiveness,

Shows a corrugated picture

Of what I see.

When the wind awakens and joins us,

The portrait will be erased;

And all that is left is wonder.

Where is reality to be found

When what was and what is

Insist upon playing with each other?

SOULFUL

Ah, said the court, don't you see?

A corporation is a person, and so,

it is absolutely free to speak.

Money to candidates is conversation.

Well, then, is it also true that a person

Is a corporation—interested primarily

In the bottom line? Guided by a profit?

Knowing that more is better?

A person, according to C.S. Lewis,

Is a soul that has a body.

But a corporation is a body

Which has no soul.

Soulful bodies delight in enough,

Having no craving for more.

Souls get hurt when they incorporate

Instead of embody.

THE MOURNING

Sometimes in the mourning

There is a glimpse of what might be

If one tried harder

      Or smarter

      Or better

      Or differently.

The "if" holds the soul as hostage

And darkens dreams.

It is then that the promise

Becomes a presence.

      Light flickers from darkness

      Power churns from weakness

      Life respirates from death;

Enlivening a worn spirit.

After resolve is exhausted

And self-reliance spent,

      Life is then set free

      By being handed an infant

      Instead of a threat, so that

      God is discovered again.

TO A FRIEND

How does the day begin?
Sometimes I prefer "hopeless."
Its is a great prelude to despair,
And a sad welcoming of self-disgust.

How does the day begin?
Sometimes I choose happy thoughts:
Everything is a wonderful "no problem."
It is an invitation to delusion.

How does the day begin?
Sometimes it starts with sorrow
And sometimes with elation.
Why is it always all or nothing?

How does the day begin?

Always it starts with a dawn

That awakens from the night before

Inviting life to go on, day by day:

    With only gentled gratitude

      and sorrow reborn as compassion;

        With only hope tempered by truth

          And a day at a time being enough.

VISCERAL

It started with a note

Scribbled on a scrap

Of a visitor's card

In a church pew.

"Dear Jimmy, I hate you.

Love, Sally."

Honesty, in the second grade.

Dilemma is ushered in.

Later on, its us and them.

And then its only us.

Finally, its just me—

My self alone.

WIRELESS

Chimes, bells, quacks, cluck, ditties:

The atmosphere is full of particles

That are charged with sound, and

Can be heard with the Geiger-like

Gadget called a "smart" phone.

Silence is finally defeated. No need

For headphones or pocket radios

Or elevator music or shopping tunes

Or dental chair sonatas.

Even talking is silenced by texting.

Anywhere, anytime, anything:

Sound is altered consciousness,

Insulating with decibels,

Muting the world outside

And numbing the world within.

I sometimes wonder if anybody

Remembers how to whistle

Or hum or be silent

Without an AP

In a world gone wireless.

47772419R00097

Made in the USA
San Bernardino, CA
07 April 2017